Troll Tales
Teacher Resources
Oscar and the Noisy Children

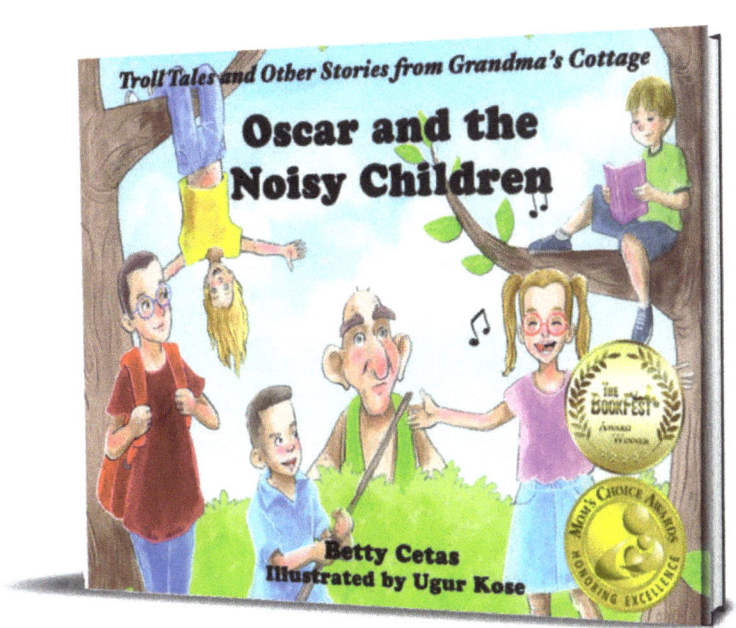

Betty Cetas
Amanda M. Cetas

Windy Sea Publishing

ISBN-13: 978-1-956277-33-3 (Print)
ISBN-13: 978-1-956277-34-0 (PDF)

Book design and cover design: Amanda Hanson
Editor: Katalena Hanson

Windy Sea Publishing, LLC
Tucson, Arizona
www.windyseapublishing.com

Table of Contents

TROLL TALES CURRICULUM
(Ages 4-8)

Overview

- **Subject Areas**: Language Arts, Music, Art, Social Studies, Science, Character Education
- **Format**: Unit study (5 Day Plan)
- **Themes**: Finnish culture, character development, nature exploration, creative storytelling
- **Tone**: Family-friendly, secular, imaginative

Unit Study: *Oscar and the Noisy Children*

Target Age: 4-8 (Preschool to 2nd Grade)

Subjects: Language Arts, Music, Art, Character Ed, Social Studies, Science

Focus Themes:

- Teamwork
- Empathy
- Problem Solving
- Nature
- Self-Awareness

Weekly Lesson Planner:

Day 1: Read the book aloud. Discuss the feelings each character portrays (Oscar's shyness, Nathaniel's hurt and anger, Jeremiah's annoyance, Adriana's desire for peace-making, etc.) and how the characters work together to solve the problem.

Day 2: Simple Physics Experiment: *Can You Help Pull Nathaniel Out?*

Day 3: Social-Emotional Learning: *Helping, Healing, and Being Heard*

Day 4: Social Studies Lesson: *Working Together in Our Community*

Day 5: Music & Movement: *Oscar's Noisy Forest*

Printables Included:

- Pulley Diagram & Science Experiment Observation Worksheet
- Feelings Chart & Oscar's Reflection Sheet
- Community Helper Worksheet
- Oscar's Kindness Pledge
- Sequencing Cards & Helper Role Cards

Course Disciplines

Language Arts Activities

- Comprehension discussion questions
- Story Sequencing Cards: "What happened first, next, last?"
- Character Reflection Journals: "How did Nathaniel feel? Why? What would you do if you were Oscar?"
- Creative writing prompt: "A time I helped someone" or "If I found someone stuck in the mud …"

Science & Nature

- Nature Walk: Look and listen for sounds that occur. Find a place to sit quietly and write down the sounds you hear. What's "noisy"? What's "quiet"?
- Mud Science: Explore how mud forms with soil + water experiments. Observe textures, temperature, drying.
- Help Pull Nathaniel Out of the Mud: Learn how a pulley system can make lifting easier.

Social-Emotional Learning (SEL)

- Discuss situations when students felt hurt, angry, left out, or helpful.
- Kindness Role-Play: Practice helping vs ignoring; how to invite others to join
- Teamwork Challenge: Work in groups to build a "rescue plan" with classroom supplies

Social Studies

- Discuss what a community is.
- Community circle map: Explain the connections between people in a community.
- Learn about the roles different people play in a community.

Music & Movement

- Quiet vs Noisy Sound Sort: Create a simple percussion rhythm with "quiet" and "noisy" instruments.
- Muddy Movement Game: Obstacle course simulating the sticky rescue mission.
- Team Rhythm Circle: Collaborate to make a rhythm with different instruments or body percussion.

Final Project Ideas

- Write a new Oscar adventure featuring one or more of the children.
- Recreate a scene from *Oscar and the Noisy Children* as a diorama.
- Create a "Candyland" style board game to trace the children's path through the forest from Grandma's Cottage to Nathaniel's muddy puddle and back.

Day 1 Lesson

Objectives:

- Understand the key ideas and details from a text by asking and answering questions.
- Retell a story focusing on the main ideas.

1. Read the book, *Oscar and the Noisy Children*, aloud.

2. Discuss the following questions.

- How did Nathaniel feel? Why?
- Why was Oscar afraid to help Nathaniel?
- What did he do to help Nathaniel?
- What role did each of the other four children play in rescuing Nathaniel?

3. Sequencing Cards

Cut out the sequencing cards and have students put them in the right order. Which three scenes happened first? Which three came next? Which three came last?

4. Character Reflection Journals

Create a booklet by folding several blank pages in half and stapling them together. Have students respond to the following prompts.

- How did Nathaniel feel? Why?
- Have you ever felt like Nathaniel did? What did you do?
- What would you do if you were Oscar in this situation?
- **Optional creative writing prompt:**
  - "A time I helped someone"
  - "If I found someone stuck in the mud …"

Note: Students can write their answers in the booklet, or they can draw images that answer the questions, depending upon their abilities.

Day 2 Lesson

Can You Help Pull Nathaniel Out?

Topic: Introduction to Pulleys
Focus: Simple machines · Force · Teamwork

Objective:

Children will learn how a **pulley makes lifting things easier** and apply the idea to helping "rescue" a stuck friend (just like Oscar and the kids helped Nathaniel).

Materials:

- A **rope or thick string** (5–6 feet long)
- A **small bucket or basket**
- A **pulley** (can use a plastic clothesline pulley, curtain pulley, or even a spool hung on a rod)
- A **chair or broomstick** (to elevate the pulley)
- **Small objects** to lift that fit in your bucket or basket (e.g., small toy, stuffed animal, bag of cotton balls)
- **Optional:** a drawing of "Nathaniel" to place in the basket!

Setup

1. Hang the pulley from the back of a chair, on a broomstick across two chairs, or from a low-hanging hook.
2. Thread the rope through the pulley.
3. Attach one end of the rope to the basket or bucket.

Put a small toy or stuffed animal in the bucket to represent Nathaniel.

(See Pulley Diagram 1.)

NOTE: If it is too easy to lift the basket or bucket, you may want to add more weight to it. It should be noticeably more difficult to lift the basket without the aid of the pulley.

Experiment Steps:

Step 1: Try lifting the bucket without the pulley.

- Let the child lift the basket straight up by the handle.
- Ask: "Was that easy or hard?"

Step 2: Now use the pulley!

- Pull the rope through the pulley to lift the basket.
- Ask: "Did it feel easier this time? Why?"

Step 3: Add Weight

- Add a small toy or two and try again.
- Let them feel the difference with and without the pulley.

Discussion Questions:

- What changed when we used the pulley?
- Why might Oscar and the children have needed teamwork to pull Nathaniel out?
- How does a pulley help us work together?

NOTE: Using a pulley changes the direction of the lifting force from straight up to a more horizontal angle. In doing this, you gain leverage by using a horizontal arm, which allows you to lift more weight with less effort.

For older students, you could include that by using two pulleys it will distribute the weight more, allowing someone to lift twice as much, but the rope will have to be pulled twice as far. One pulley attached to the bucket and another hanging from the broom handle. The rope goes over the broom handle, down through the pulley on the bucket, then back up through the top pulley, and out to the person pulling. (See Pulley Diagram 2.)

Draw what you built!

In the space provided on your Science Experiment Observation Sheet, allow time for kids to draw their pulley system and what they lifted.

Optional Extension Activity

Give the kids two ropes and two pulleys and let them "race" to pull their buckets up the fastest — teamwork encouraged!

Day 3 Lesson

Helping, Healing, and Being Heard

Topic: Empathy, Self-regulation, Inclusion, Collaboration
Duration: 30-40 minutes

SEL Competencies: Empathy, Social Awareness, Relationship Skills, Responsible Decision-Making

Objectives

By the end of the lesson, students will be able to:

- Recognize feelings like **anger**, **loneliness**, and **concern for others**.

- Identify ways to **include others** and **ask for help**.

- Practice **teamwork** and **problem-solving** through discussion and role-play.

- Practice **empathy** through storytelling, role-play, and reflection.

Lesson Outline

1. Warm-Up: *How Did They Feel?* (5–7 minutes)

Materials: Emotion cards or puppet faces, storybook, chart paper

1. Read or review the story briefly.

2. Ask:

   - "How did Nathaniel feel when he was left behind?"

   - "How do you think Oscar felt watching from the woods?"

   - "How do you think the other children felt when they saw Nathaniel stuck?"

Chart the feelings using the Feelings Chart provided.

Alternatively: Use the Oscar's Reflection Sheet provided.

2. Discussion: *Why Did They Work Together?* (10 minutes)

Ask:

- What would have happened if no one helped Nathaniel?
- Was it hard for Oscar to step up to help? Why?
- Have you ever felt nervous to help or ask for help?

Draw Parallels:

- What could you do if you saw someone who was left out at recess?
- What can we say to invite others to play?
- What could we do if we are feeling left-out?

Introduce **kindness scripts:**

- Do you want to play with us?
- I noticed you looked sad – can I help?
- Let's ask an adult if we're not sure what to do.

3. Interactive Activity: *Rescue Role-Play* (10–15 minutes)

Set Up: Use classroom space as "Oscar's forest." Give one child a "mud spot" to sit in. Others are the helpers.

Instructions:

- Role-play one child getting stuck.
- Another is shy (like Oscar) and needs to decide how to help.
- Others come back and work together to "rescue" their friend using materials they can find in the classroom.

After the role-play, ask:

- "What worked well?"
- "Was it easier when we worked together, or individually?"
- "What made Oscar brave?"

4. Creative Reflection: *Kindness Tree or Tool Kit* (optional) (10 minutes)

Choose one:

- **Kindness Tree:** Each child adds a paper leaf with one way to include or help others.
- **Teamwork Tool Kit:** Draw or write things you can "use" to help someone (kind words, listening ears, helping hands).

5. Closing Thought

Ask:

- "What is one kind thing you could do if someone feels left out?"
- "How can we be like Oscar *and* the children in this story?"

Optional Extension:

Have students repeat the Classroom Kindness Pledge and sign their names. Then display the pledge somewhere in the classroom to remind students to be kind.

Day 4 Lesson

Working Together in Our Community

Duration: 30-40 minutes
Focus: Inclusion · Helping others · Group responsibility · Roles in a community

Objectives

Students will:

- Understand what a community is and why cooperation is important.
- Recognize that people have different roles and strengths.
- Identify ways they can help others in their classroom and neighborhoods.
- Reflect on what it means to include everyone and not leave someone behind.

Lesson Outline

1. Introduction: *What is a Community?* (5 minutes)

Ask:

- "What is a community?"
- "Who is in our community?" (e.g. family, classmates, teachers, helpers)

Tie to the story:

"Oscar lives in a forest community of animals. The children visited it. When someone got stuck, the group had **to work together** to help him."

Create a class **list of community helpers**. (Fire fighter, teacher, policeman, neighbor, friend, troll(!), etc.)

2. Activity 1: *Community Circle Map* (10–12 minutes)

Materials:

Large paper or whiteboard, markers

Steps:

1. Draw Oscar in the center of the circle map.
2. Around him draw and label:
   - Nathaniel
   - The four other children

- Animals and other helpers, who are part of his forest
- "Help!" speech bubble and other appropriate speech bubbles
- Forest features or other tools used to help

Ask:

- "Who helped Nathaniel?"
- "Could one person do it all?"
- "What did each person bring to the rescue?"

As students answer the questions above, draw lines to make connections between the elements on the circle map.

Emphasize how different skills (bravery, speaking up, strength, awareness) all helped solve the problem.

3. Activity 2: *What's My Role?* (10-15 minutes)

Materials: Picture cards (found on pages 25-29) or drawings of different roles (rescuers, helpers, friends)

Instructions:

- Assign roles to small groups or partners:
  - "You're Oscar—how do you help?"
  - "You're the one who saw someone was left out—what do you say?"
  - "You're a helper—what can you do that's kind?"

Children act out or describe their part in a simple skit or puppet show.

After the skit or show, students will each complete the Community Helper Reflection Worksheet.

4. Reflection Activity (5–7 minutes)

Prompt:

"Have you ever been part of a group that helped someone?"

Let children draw or write (dictation works for younger kids):

- "I helped someone by…"
- "I felt proud when…"
- "Next time I see someone who needs help, I will…"

5. Optional Extension: *Real-World Helpers*

Introduce real-world community helpers: fire fighters, nurses, crossing guards, police, coaches, neighbors, people passing by.

Ask: "How do they help?"

Day 5 Lesson

Oscar's Noisy Forest

Duration: 30-40 minutes
Focus: Sound exploration · Body control · Rhythm · Emotion expression · Group cooperation

Objectives

Children will:

- Identify and explore **noisy** and **quiet** sounds
- Move their bodies to express character feelings and story events
- Practice **working together** through musical play
- Build awareness of sound, space, and group dynamics

1. Warm-up: *Noisy or Quiet?* (5-7 minutes)

Materials: rhythm sticks, shaker eggs, scarves, or hands

1. Introduce Oscar's forest as a quiet place.
2. Make sound examples:
   - Clap softly = rustling leaves 🌿
   - Tap loudly = children stomping through the woods 👣
   - Shake fast = scared and frantic 😱
   - Tap slow = calm and helpful 🤝

Call out: "Oscar's forest is..." (quiet/noisy) and have kids respond with matching body sounds.

2. Activity 1: *Musical Story Walk* (8-10 minutes)

Set up a musical retelling with movement.

Use live instruments or simple recorded sounds.

- **March**: The children enter the forest. Stomp to a steady beat.
- **Freeze**: Nathaniel is left behind. Pause and make a "confused" pose.
- **Wiggle/Slide**: He gets stuck in the mud. Sway and sink slowly to the floor.
- **Tiptoe**: Oscar tries to help—move quietly and gently.
- **Group Pull**: Everyone helps—join hands and lean backward together as if pulling.

Ask: "What kind of music matches each part? Fast? Slow? Loud? Soft?"

3. Activity 2: *Feelings Freeze Dance* (5-7 minutes)

Play music with changing tempos or use a playlist.

- When the music stops, call out a feeling:

- o "Sad!" → slump and sigh
- o "Happy!" → jump and wave
- o "Left out!" → turn away and curl up
- o "Helpful!" → stretch out a hand
- Children freeze in the matching shape or expression.

Reinforce that **we all feel different things**, and that it's okay!

4. Activity 3: *Team Rhythm Circle* (5-10 minutes)

Use percussion or body rhythm.

1. Each child takes a turn adding a sound or beat.
2. Pass the rhythm around like a "rescue rope"—building a musical chain.
3. For a challenge: assign each child a "role" (soft shaker = Oscar, stomper = child, tapper = mud).

Encourage listening, turn-taking, and group awareness.

5. Cool Down & Reflection (3-5 minutes)

- Lie on the floor or sit quietly.
- Play soft forest sounds or quiet music.
- Ask:
  - o "What part of Oscar's forest would you want to visit?"
  - o "What sound or movement made you feel helpful?"

Bonus Extension (Optional)

- Let children **draw their favorite part of the musical forest**
- Or make **"forest rhythm sticks"** from cardboard tubes or nature items

Additional Unit Ideas

Story Time & Discussion

- Read aloud or listen to the story multiple times throughout the week.
- Discuss main characters, setting, and the problem/solution.
- Discuss applications to personal situations.

Questions to ask:

- What was your favorite part?
- How did the characters feel? How did they change?
- What would you do if you were in this story?

Language Arts Focus

- **Vocabulary Words**: Choose 3–5 new or fun words from the story (e.g., sensitive, whirlwind, peacemaker, comfortable, observant).
- **Comprehension**: Simple Q&A, sequencing activities, retelling in own words.
- **Creative Writing Prompt** (adapt by age):
    - Draw and write your own troll character.
    - "What would I do if I saw someone who needed help?"
    - Finish the sentence: "Oscar was afraid of Nathaniel because…"

Cultural Connection – Finland

- Introduce Finland on the map. Compare it to your location.
- Research fun facts: language, landscapes, animals (lynx, reindeer, bears), weather.
- Basic intro to Finnish folklore traditions (neutral tone).

Science or Nature Study

- Identify one animal or plant that is typical of Finnish forests or lakes.
- Study animal habits, habitats, and behaviors.
- Go on a local nature walk: "What would live in our ecosystem (environment)?"
- Visit an aquarium to learn about the fish and animals that live in lakes and rivers.

Art & Expression

- Scene Diorama: Build a scene from the story with a paper or cardboard base, or shoebox.
- Mud Print Art: Use brown paint and texture tools to simulate muddy "footprints."
- Character Puppets: Create Oscar and the children to retell the story as a puppet play.

Character Building & Social-Emotional Learning

- Discuss themes like kindness, bravery, honesty, or problem-solving.
- Role-play scenes: "What would be a kind thing to do?"
- Draw a "Feelings Forest" where each tree represents a different emotion.

Final Project

- Draw a favorite scene from the story and explain why it is a favorite.
- Short puppet show retelling the story.
- Create a safety poster warning people of possible dangers in your neighborhood or the area in which your student(s) life.

Pulley Diagrams for the Science Experiment

Diagram 1: Showing the Use of One Pulley

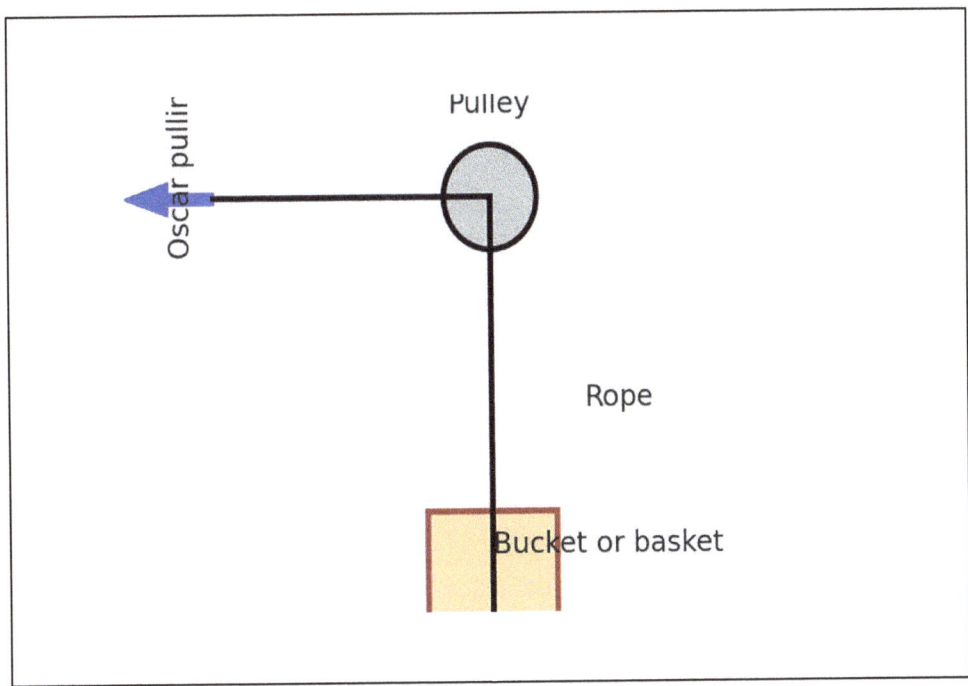

Diagram 2: Showing the Use of Two Pullies (Block & Tackle System)

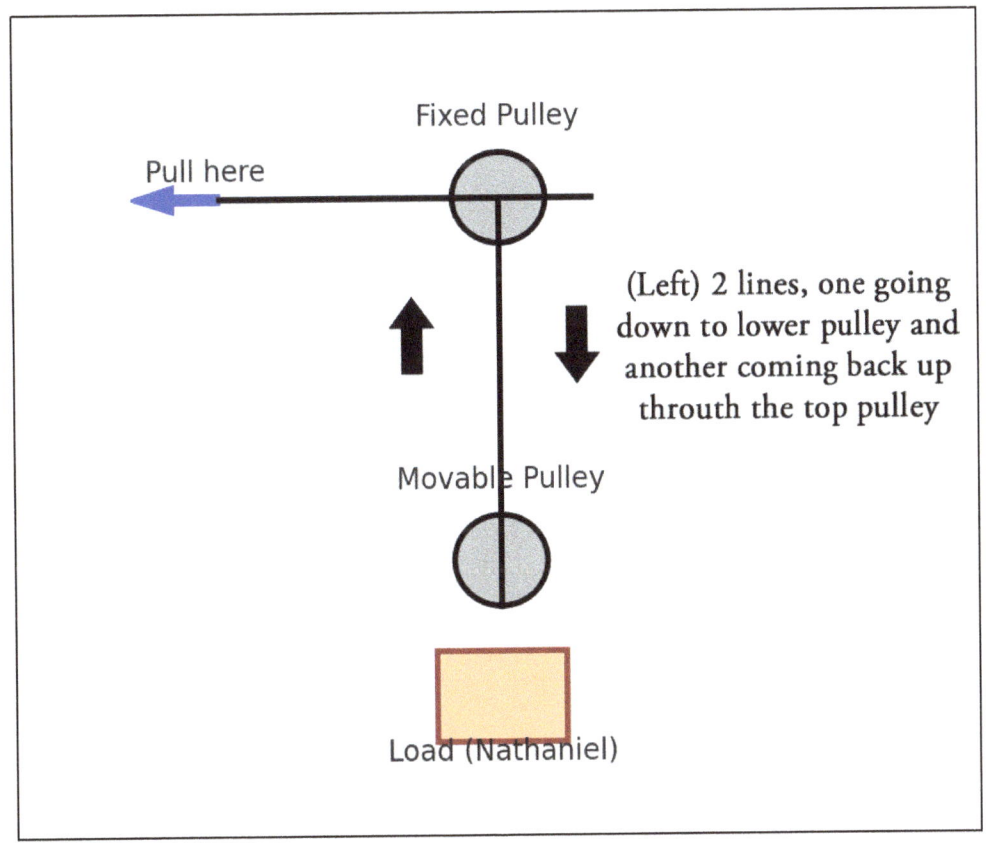

Science Experiment Observation Sheet

Can You Help Pull Nathaniel Out?

In this experiment, we will see what happens when we use a pulley to help lift heavy things.

What effect do you predict the pulley will have on lifting an object?

I predict _____

_____

Materials I Used:

☐ A rope or thick string (about 5-6 feet long)
☐ A small basket or bucket
☐ A pulley (or spool, curtain ring, clothesline wheel)
☐ A chair, broomstick, or similar stand
☐ Small toys (to represent Nathaniel)
☐ Optional: light toys or coins for added weight

Setup Instructions

1. Hang your pulley on the back of a chair or across a broomstick between two chairs. (Thread a string through the spool and tie each end of the string to the top of the chair or broomstick.)

2. Thread your rope through the pulley.

3. Tie one end of the rope to a basket or bucket.

4. Place a small toy inside.

What to Do

1. Try to lift the basket straight up without the pulley. How does it feel?

2. Now try using the pulley to pull the rope. (Feed the rope over the spool.) What is different?

3. Try adding more toys and lifting again. Is it easier with the pulley, or not?

Reflection Questions

What changed when you used the pulley? _____

_____

Did the pulley help you, or not? Explain. _____

_____

What was the benefit of the children working together to lift Nathaiel? Explain. _____

_____

_____

Draw Your Pulley Rescue:

[Draw a picture of your pulley helping lift Nathaniel out of the mud!]

```



```

What I Learned:

Pulleys are helpful because _____

_____

_____

Feelings Chart

WHO	How They Felt (in words)	Draw a Simple Face to Show How They Felt
Nathaniel		
Oscar		
Jeremiah		
Adriana		
Isabelle		
Elijah		

www.windyseapublishing.com   Windy Sea Publishing

Oscar's Reflection Sheet

How Did They Feel?

Circle the feelings the character might have had. You can circle more than one.

Oscar: Worried   Happy   Sad   Helpful

Nathaniel: Angry   Sad   Calm   Scared

Other Children: Excited   Surprised   Glad   Sorry

My Thoughts

How would you feel if you got left behind like Nathaniel?

_____

_____

What can you say or do to help someone who feels left out?

_____

_____

Draw and Share

Community Helper Reflection Worksheet

1. Which helper role did you have (or like best)?

Oscar the Observer

Nathaniel the Needer   Elijah the Helper

Jeremiah the Planner   The Listener

Adriana the Encourager   The Cheerleader

Isabelle the Doer   The Friend

I chose: _____

2. What did you do to help your team or friend?

_____

_____

3. How did it feel to help or be helped?

Happy   Calm   Nervous   Proud   A little sad

I felt: _____

4. Next time, how can you help someone in need?

_____

_____

Draw a time you helped someone or were helped.

Oscar's Kindness Pledge

In our classroom, we choose kindness.

We listen when someone needs a voice.
We speak up when someone feels left out.
We share, include, and help each other.
We celebrate what makes us different.
We work together to solve problems.

We are a team. We are kind. We are strong.

Sign below to show your promise:

Sequencing Cards

Cut out the cards and shuffle them. Then have students order them in the correct sequence (three scenes for the beginning, three for the middle, and three for the end).

All images by Ugur Kose © Windy Sea Publishing, LLC

Helper Role Cards

Cut out the cards, front and back together, as one unit. Fold the card in the middle and tape it closed. Use these cards with the Day 4 Lesson.

Oscar the Observer

Watches quietly and notices when someone needs help.

Nathaniel the Needer

Needs help and learns it's okay to ask.

Jeremiah the Planner

Thinks of ideas for how the group can work together.

Adriana the Encourager

Says kind words and reminds others to keep trying.

Isabelle the Doer

Helps by pulling, lifting, or taking action.

Elijah the Helper

Helps to find what is needed to help.

All images by Ugur Kose © Windy Sea Publishing, LLC

The Listener

Stops to hear what someone else is feeling or needing.

The Friend

Includes others and makes sure no one feels left out.

The Cheerleader

Claps and cheers to encourage everyone to keep going.

All images by Ugur Kose © Windy Sea Publishing, LLC

About the Authors

Betty Cetas taught first and second grades for several years until moving to Australia with her husband. After returning to the United States, she continued teaching in Sunday school classes, Bible studies, and imparting life lessons through her stories. She enjoys traveling and especially loved the log cottage she bought in the remote woods of Finland, where she spent summers with her family and friends, telling fanciful stories of provincial trolls, shy moose, and impish fish. She lives in Tucson, AZ with her husband and little dog, Abby, and summers in the woods in Williams, AZ.

Amanda M. Cetas is the author of the award-winning historical fiction adventure series, *A Country for Castoffs.* She was inspired to write these stories from two decades of researching her own family history. She taught diverse grade-level and Advanced Placement courses in American, European and world history to high school and middle school students for fourteen years. Amanda lives with her husband and two little Yorkie mixes. She has three grown children and four amazing grandchildren to keep her active!

Other books with accompanying teacher resources

Ages 4-8:

Oscar and the Awful, Horrible Smell
Oscar and Otto
Moe and the Tree Climbers (Coming Summer 2025)
Otto and the Lost Children (Coming Spring 2026)

Middle Grade/Young Adult:

Thrown to the Wind (Ages 9-12)
A Home in the Wilderness (11-13)
At the Mercy of the Sea (YA)
Charting a New Course (Coming in 2026)